ISBN 978-1-5278-5115-3
PIBN 10891073

# 1 MONTH OF
# FREE
# READING

at

## www.ForgottenBooks.com

By purchasing this book you are eligible for one month membership to ForgottenBooks.com, giving you unlimited access to our entire collection of over 1,000,000 titles via our web site and mobile apps.

To claim your free month visit:
www.forgottenbooks.com/free891073

English
Français
Deutsche
Italiano
Español
Português

# www.forgottenbooks.com

**Mythology** Photography **Fiction**
Fishing Christianity **Art** Cooking
Essays Buddhism Freemasonry
Medicine **Biology** Music **Ancient
Egypt** Evolution Carpentry Physics
Dance Geology **Mathematics** Fitness
Shakespeare **Folklore** Yoga Marketing
**Confidence** Immortality Biographies
Poetry **Psychology** Witchcraft
Electronics Chemistry History **Law**
Accounting **Philosophy** Anthropology
Alchemy Drama Quantum Mechanics
Atheism Sexual Health **Ancient History**
**Entrepreneurship** Languages Sport
Paleontology Needlework Islam
**Metaphysics** Investment Archaeology
Parenting Statistics Criminology
**Motivational**

# CIHM/ICMH
Microfiche
Series.

# CIHM/ICMH
Collection de
microfiches.

Canadian Institute for Historical Microreproductions / Institut canadien de microreproductions his

## Technical and Bibliographic Notes/Notes techniques et bibliographiques

The Institute has attempted to obtain the best original copy available for filming. Features of this copy which may be bibliographically unique, which may alter any of the images in the reproduction, or which may significantly change the usual method of filming, are checked below.

L'Institut a microfilmé le meill qu'il lui a été possible de se pr de cet exemplaire qui sont peu point de vue bibliographique, une image reproduite, ou qui modification dans la méthode sont indiqués ci-dessous.

☐ Coloured covers/
Couverture de couleur

☐ Covers damaged/
Couverture endommagée

☐ Covers restored and/or laminated/
Couverture restaurée et/ou pelliculée

☐ Cover title missing/
Le titre de couverture manque

☐ Coloured maps/
Cartes géographiques en couleur

☐ Coloured ink (i.e. other than blue or black)/
Encre de couleur (i.e. autre que bleue ou noire)

☐ Coloured plates and/or illustrations/
Planches et/ou illustrations en couleur

☐ Bound with other material/
Relié avec d'autres documents

☐ Tight binding may cause shadows or distortion along interior margin/
La re liure serrée peut causer de l'ombre ou de la distorsion le long de la marge intérieure

☐ Blank leaves added during restoration may appear within the text. Whenever possible, these have been omitted from filming/
Il se peut que certaines pages blanches ajoutées lors d'une restauration apparaissent dans le texte, mais, lorsque cela était possible, ces pages n'ont pas été filmées.

☐ Additional comments:/
Commentaires supplémentaires:

☐ Coloured pages/
Pages de couleur

☐ Pages damaged/
Pages endommagées

☐ Pages restored and/or la
Pages restaurées et/ou p

☑ Pages discoloured, staine
Pages décolorées, tachet

☐ Pages detached/
Pages détachées

☐ Showthrough/
Transparence

☐ Quality of print varies/
Qualité inégale de l'impre

☑ Includes supplementary
Comprend du matériel su

☐ Only edition available/
Seule édition disponible

☐ Pages wholly or partially
slips, tissues, etc., have
ensure tha best possible
Les pages totalement ou
obscurcies par un feuillet
etc., ont été filmées à no
obtenir la meilleure imag

here has been reproduced thanks
ty of:

Ontario

earing here are the best quality
ering the condition and legibility
opy and in keeping with the
t specifications.

Les images suivantes ont été reproduites avec le
plus grand soin, compte tenu de la condition et
de la netteté de l'exemplaire filmé, et en
conformité avec les conditions du contrat de
filmage.

in printed paper covers are filmed
the front cover and ending on
ith a printed or illustrated impres-
k cover when appropriate. All
opies are filmed beginning on the
a printed or illustrated impres-
g on the last page with a printed
pression.

Les exemplaires originaux dont la couverture en
papier est imprimée sont filmés en commençant
par le premier plat et en terminant soit par la
dernière page qui comporte une empreinte
d'impression ou d'illustration, soit par le second
plat, selon le cas. Tous les autres exemplaires
originaux sont filmés en commençant par la
première page qui comporte une empreinte
d'impression ou d'illustration et en terminant par
la dernière page qui comporte une telle
empreinte.

ed frame on each microfiche
e symbol ➡ (meaning "CON-
e symbol ▽ (meaning "END"),
ies.

Un des symboles suivants apparaîtra sur la
dernière image de chaque microfiche, selon le
cas: le symbole ➡ signifie "A SUIVRE", le
symbole ▽ signifie "FIN".

harts, etc., may be filmed at
tion ratios. Those too large to be
d in one exposure are filmed
e upper left hand corner, left to
bottom, as many frames as
llowing diagrams illustrate the

Les cartes, planches, tableaux, etc., peuvent être
filmés à des taux de réduction différents.
Lorsque le document est trop grand pour être
reprod  en un seul cliché, il est filmé à partir
de l'a  supérieur gauche, de gauche à droite,
et de  t en bas, en prenant le nombre
d'images nécessaire. Les diagrammes suivants
illustrent la méthode.

# Hunting for ~~~~~ Pictures

The story of the adventures of M.W. Bro. J. Ross
Robertson, in collecting pictures for
Masonic history.

TORONTO
George N. Morang & Company, Limited
1900

# For Illustrating Purposes.

Hunting for the proverbial needle in an up-to-date haystack is child's play compared with a search for pictures with which to illustrate history —especially Masonic history.

Not that illustrations are necessary to hold down a reader's attention in any subject—but ordinary readers are so human—so very human. They want all the good things in sight. At a hotel they eagerly scan the bill of fare for the side dishes of the artist in cooking. If they open a book they seek just as eagerly in the chapters of letter press for the interleaved illustrations that are served up by the artist in half-tone. The entrees of the chef satisfy the physical, the half-tones of the picture-maker the mental taste. Besides, pictures fix in the memory much that might without them pass into oblivion.

These thoughts recall a pleasant June afternoon on an Atlantic liner and a talk with M. W. Bro. J. Ross Robertson, the Past Grand Master of the Grand Lodge of Canada, who, as Craft readers— yes, and the Canadian world at large—know, completed a few months ago an elaborate history of Masonry in Canada.

We were enjoying a quiet afternoon—the perfection of June weather. The sun was bright; in the sky were a few fleecy clouds; the sea was without a ripple, not the semblance of a cap was to be seen. The thermometer was moving about in the sixties and the barometer, so the deck steward said, promised Queen's weather. As the liner cut through the water at a—to be exact—five-hundred-and three-mile a day rate, we looked seaward, resting on our deck chairs and talked of Masonry in Canada. Yes, and if the reader of this chat be historically inclined, he may amplify his knowledge of Craft work in Canada quite readily by a reading of Bro. Robertson's massive volumes.

It is not Bro. Robertson's history of the Craft that leads me to this write-up—the letter press I'll leave fu. another time.

To-day, I talked to him about the pictures—yes, the pictures—400 of them—yes, nearly five, and all of them rare—every one a gem—a wealth of illustration that amazes readers, whether Craftsmen or not, and puzzles picture and print men. I asked Bro. Robertson:

"Where did these art gems come from? Where have they been hidden all the years of this century? How did you unvarth them? How did you get 2,000 pages of letter press into shape?"

"Well," said Bro. Robertson, "this liner would have to make quite a few trips across the Atlantic before it would cover the length of journeys made to give the Craft in Canada all that I have written between the covers of my two volumes. The letter press is the outcome of a close reading of not less than 30,000 pages of Masonic MSS. and general literature—historical and Masonic—stored, a lot of it, in Great Britain, some in the United States and much of it, yes the bulk of it, in Canada."

"But what a time it must have taken to get through such a mass of stuff."

"It certainly did take time, but truth, not time

was the essence of the contract. I wanted facts, all capable of proof by documentary evidence—no filmy tradition, and, therefore, the time occupied would run into years, say sixteen, for the letter press, and of that sixteen a couple for the pictures. When I say this I am trying to make a good guess. Fancy a month at a time in London in the British Museum and weeks in old print shops searching for pictures."

"But there must have been a lot of incidents in your researches. You did not order up a picture just as you would order your dinner on this Atlantic service."

"No, indeed. I was nearly a month on the search before I captured the print of the Vanguard. I'll tell you about that picture later on. As for incidents, my hunt was full of incidents. The trouble was that there were so many hunts, just bristling with incident. When I look at some of the reproductions I have to smile at the ins and outs of that particular hunt cross my mind. I have had queer experiences. I have, as the small boy would say in hide-and-seek, been hot and cold in my quest for pictures. What disappointments I have had just when ready to land a print, month after month, yes, year after year, like a detective on a trail, and then in the end to know that I might as well have tried to grasp a shadow on the wall."

"But you have had a lot of success. Four or five hundred engravings are not bound up inside of two thousand printed pages without some effort. especially when three-fourths are from originals."

"That's true enough. The fact is that I have spent months at a time in the best libraries of the old world, the National Library at Paris, the British Museum in London, and that of the Grand Lodge of England in Great Queen street, London—the centre from which all Craft Masonry in England radiates. All these are good libraries. For MSS. and prints the British libraries are far in advance. The National Library in Paris has but little Canadian—either in books, MSS. or print. It has one set of Bartlett's sketches which are not all rare. Many of them can be bought for a penny apiece in London. It has also a few lithos of Halifax, N.S., engraved during the eighteenth century."

" How about British collections?"

" Well, of works concerning Canada the great museum in London has a fair collection—that is fair when compared with the unique collection in the Public Library at Toronto and the Parliamentary Library at Ottawa. In drawings, engravings and photographs the Museum is rich. Its print room is a treasure fold. The pleasant weeks I have spent in sixteen years in the print room and in the great circular reading room brought me ample return."

" Where did you find the Vanguard print?"

" In the print room of the Museum. The Vanguard was the ship on which Bro. Dunckerley held a lodge at Quebec in 1760. I had almost given that chase up. I had explored the print and model room of the Royal United Service Institution opposite the Horse Guards and examined every naval history in its book shelves that had a picture, spent a long day at Greenwich Hospital examining models of men-of-war from 1650 and photographing oil paintings of groups of war-ships that might contain the Vanguard, for I couldn't take the oils away and therefore had to submit the photos to an expert. But all in vain. I thought I had the ship in an oil painting showing the fire fleet of the French attempting to pass through the British fleet off Quebec in 1759, but my expert friend said I was on the wrong track. So my effort in that direction came to an untimely end.'

" What was your next try ? "

" Well, I knew that the Vanguard was at Quebec in 1758 and again in 1759, and 1 remembered seeing some engravings of Quebec and the St. Lawrence with men-of-war in the stream, made in 1759-60 by Capt. Harvey Smyth, one of Wolfe's aides.

" These engravings were in the print room of the British Museum. One engraving had a view of Quebec made by Smyth on board the Vanguard and in this picture were two men-of-war lying in front of the city. These engravings I had photo-graphed. In the original engravings these ships are about tl     ·ıı ·ı ters of an inch long. 1 enlarged them to thrє          for better examination, яо as to see if the .            :e ship and number of guns carried corresı.            'h the printed and MSS. descrip-ticns I .            :er. But all to no purpose. My expert frieъ..      10, by the way, can tell you the build of every ship in the navy from the earliest days, pointed to the flags each ship was flying. One had the admiral's flag, the other the vice-admiral's flag, and as neither the admiral nor his vice was on the Vanguard that settled my search as far as that picture was concerned."

" Did you despair ? "

" No, I did not. I had another look at the print room catalogue and found companion engravings, one a ship of war entering Wolfe's Cove, near Que-bec, and another of a ship of war passing the Pierced Rock on the Gaspe coast. I examined both and to my delight I found that the last-named picture had been made by Capt. Harvey Smyth prior to 1760, while in the Vanguard as she passed the Pierced Rock on her way to England. This looked near my goal. Once more I made use of the camera. I reproduced the picture in enlarged form and my cup of satisfaction overflowed when my expert friend told me that the ship was undoubtedly the long-sought Vanguard. But this did not satisfy me. I knew that if the Vanguard was off the Pierced Rock in 1758 her log would give me the day and date."

" Her log, did you say?"

" Yes, her log. Fancy seeking for the log of a British man-of-war that floated in the St. Lawrence in 1758."

" The actual MSS. log?"

" Yes. England is a wonderful country and London is not so slow a town. It has its wealth in gold and in MSS. records—no other city in the world has the same. It was not to the Museum nor any library that I sped this time—no, but to the Public Record Office in Chancery Lane—the great storehouse of official MSS. I entered its examining room, wrote my wants on a slip of paper —a printed form—handed it to an attendant, and before I was fairly seated at the table waiting for an answer, the attendant, with a ponderous volume, weighing pounds, planted on the table the original log of the Vanguard for 1758 and the entry in the handwriting of the officer of the day, showing that the Vanguard was in Gaspe Bay on the 5th Sept., and off the Pierced Rock on the 20th Sept., 1758. That's how I found the Vanguard."

" Did you make many Canadian historical finds in your hunt for Masonic pictures?"

" Yes, quite a number, some very important. For instance, one day while I was searching in the King's Library in the British Museum, I opened a portfolio that was a revelation to me and to all who now know of it. It was a collection of original drawings of Canadian views and scenes by Mrs. Simcoe, wife of Sir John Graves Simcoe, Governor of Upper Canada, 1792-7—a welcome find. No one seemed to have dropped on to it, although it was presented by the Governor to King George III. in 1800, and has been for nearly a century in the library. The portfolio had thirty-two pictures of part of Canada by the actual hand of Mrs. Simcoe during her sojourn in Canada. Many were bits of land and waterscape on the lakes of old Upper Canada, some were views of towns and town sites; Kingston in 1792, Toronto Harbour in 1792, showing the shores from the garrison east to the Don. Another of the Mohawk village on the Grand River, with the Indian Council House and the house of Capt. John Brant. It '., 'he only picture extant of the original village. Nuth'ng stands to-day except the old church. This picture is unique, for it shows the original elevation of the church with the spire at its east end. In 1829 the church was renovated, the sr're taken down and rebuilt at the west end instead of at the east and the entrance to the church was changed from the east to the west end. Then in this collection I found a picture of Navy Hall, Governor Simcoe's residence at the mouth of the Niagara River, and a capital view of Queenston with the barracks of the Queen's Rangers. This regiment had an early and well worked lodge, when it was stationed at York in 1798. The lodge room was in one of the row cf log houses at the east end of the Fort, which, however, was not burnt in ·1812."

"What about the Grand Lodge Library in London?"

"The Grand Lodge of England has a good library at Freemasons' Hall, and Bro. Sadler, the Grand Sub-Librarian, has a fine collection of Masonic prints and engravings. Sadler's work 'n and for that library could not be repaid in gold. He knows every book, cover to cover, and the MSS. and prints are to him as household words. The old brother is a walking Craft encyclopedia. I shall always appreciate his help in my work."

"I heard you say at a lodge meeting in Toronto some years ago, that you had a lively search after the faces of some of the early Provincial Grand Masters of Canada?"

"Yes, the past rulers of the Craft in Canada from 1759 down to 1845 have in a way been a source of anxiety to me. I have been for years on the look-out for pictures of two or three, like Lieut. Guinnett, of Lodge No. 192, Irish Register, in the 47th Regiment—the first Provincial Grand Master at Quebec in 1759—or Col. Simon Fraser, son of old Lord Lovat. Fraser installed the officers of the lodges in the Ancient City, in June, 1760. Then Bro. Spanner of the 28th Regiment, acted in 1761, Bro. Milbourne West, followed by Lieut. Turner, both of the 47th. I have never been able to find a portrait of any of these brethren, nor of Bro. John Collins (you know John Collins? It's popular nowadays, more easily found than the picture of the old Provincial Grand Masters). Another picture that I looked in vain for, was that of Col. Christopher Carleton, a nephew of Sir Guy Carleton. He was in the 29th Foot and was Provincial Grand Master in 1786 at Quebec. He died and was buried there. But my efforts were unsuccessful. The late Lord Dorchester diligently sought, at my request, for his ancestor's picture in the archives and picture rooms of the Carleton family, but without avail. He said that it never had been painted—certainly it had never been engraved. Bros. Guinnett, Fraser, West, Spanner and Turner were on Abraham's Plains with Wolfe. These were the men who held the Craft together in Quebec from 1759-63.

"The most valuable find in connection with Masonry in Quebec about 1761, was the Craft certificate of Lieut. James Leslie, of Select Lodge at Quebec. I have to thank Bro. J. B. McLean, of Montreal, for the tip as to this picture. He knew that I was keen for old Quebec documents, for I had told him of the finding of three sheets of the minutes of the Grand Lodge of Quebec of 1781, in the waste paper basket of a bookbinder's shop in Quebec about 1800. Capt. Norman Leslie allowed me to reproduce his ancestor's certificate. Bro. W. J. Hughan says that certificate and the warrant of the lodge at Detroit in 1764, are two of the most valuable finds ever made in connection with Masonry in America.

"In my quests in Britain I had quite an experience, particularly in searching for Bro. Simon McGillivray's portrait. You know he was the brother who came to York (Toronto) in 1822, and by order of the Duke of Sussex, reorganized the Craft in Upper Canada.

"All that I knew of McGillivray's life and history could have been written on a ten-cent piece. He was connected with the North-west Company which preceded the Hudson Bay Company, and some one told me that he was a director of the Canada Company. The Hon. Geo. W. Allan, of Toronto, referred me to the Canada Company's office in London, England, for information. But the ignorance of the officials in that office was most profound. They knew but little. They admitted that such a man had been born, yes, had lived, and had had the honour of a directorship in the company, about seventy or eighty years ago, but this was all. They amplified this information with the fact that he was an old bachelor and had passed away without kith or kin."

"And so, Bro. Robertson, you were side-tracked again?"

"Yes, but only to switch on to the main line again, as soon as opportunity offered. I admit that I felt out of sorts at my non-success, but I soon re-built my shattered hopes and started off once more to trace the second Provincial Grand Master of old Upper Canada."

"What did you do?"

"Well, I did what I should have done at the out-set. I visited Somerset House in the Strand, and with the aid of that most serviceable coin, a British shilling, I read the will of Simon McGillivray, who died at Dartmouth Row, Blackheath, in 1840. I found that he was a son-in-law of his executor, Sir John Easthope, the proprietor of the London Morning Chronicle. But beyond that nothing more."

"Did this end your search?"

"No, I crossed the Thames, walked for miles in the neighbourhood of Blackheath, to find Dartmouth Row, but it, like McGillivray, had passed away. After a ten-mile tramp, occupying from early morning until late afternoon, calling at a dozen houses, interviewing postmasters, postmistresses and officials, and looking over old maps and plans, I gave up the search for that day."

"And did that finish your effort?"

"No, it did not. I refreshed myself with an hour's rest and then I picked up the London Directory. I wrote a letter, setting forth my wants, to the only representative of the name of McGillivray to be found in the commercial section of the directory. Then I wrote to the address of every Auldjo in the directory. I knew that McGillivray had had a cousin or relative named Auldjo, who was H. M. Consul at Gene.a for years. I posted my letters and awaited the result. The next afternoon's late post brought me a letter from the one McGillivray, stating briefly, 'I know nothing of the McGillivray you are in search of.' So that on the first round I was knocked out, but I smiled on the second round, for the next post brought me a courteous letter from a Mrs. Auldjo, of Queen's Gate, Kensington, suggesting that if I would call on Messrs. Berkley, Smith & Son, Gray's Inn, my desire for information about McGillivray would be satisfied."

"So that you had success in sight?"

"Yes. I visited the firm—a legal one—one that for

a century or so had occupied a suite of offices in Gray's Inn. A junior member received me courteously, introduced me to his father, a kindly gentleman of the old school, who listened attentively to my plaint, and, as I finished, said: ' Yes, we know the Auldjo family,' and pointing to an exquisite bust by Tassi in the corner of the room, said: ' That is a bust of Mr. Auldjo, McGillivray's cousin, when he was British Consul at Geneva.' "

'· You were fortunate indeed."

"Yes, fortunate for the time being, but my troubles were not half over. The firm said that McGillivray was a son-in-law of Sir John Easthope and that by his marriage he had had a daughter, who married sometime in the sixties, Rear Admiral Dawkins, of the British Navy. They did not know his address, but that might be obtained at the Admiralty. Yes, it ' might ' be obtained at the Admiralty. There are many very good things that might be obtained at the Admiralty, but information as to the addresses of retired British Admirals is one of the articles that are not kept on the bargain counters of that honoured institution."

" Surely they did not refuse the information?"

" No, they did not refuse. They simply declared that to give the address of a British Admiral might cause such a fracture of the rules and regulations of the Admiralty that the official, who aided or abetted in said fracture, might have to drink superannuation tea for the remainder of his life."

·' Well, you surprise me."

" Surprise you! Why it nearly took my breath away. I explained to the courteous official—a retired quartermaster—that I was not a summons-server, that I had nothing in the shape of a writ concealed on my person and that my enquiries were made with friendly, not hostile intent to the Admiral aforesaid."

" Did he soften?"

"Yes, he said I had better enquire at the Pay-master's office a few feet away. I did so, but again encountered my Nemesis. The clerk whom I addressed said that to accede to my request was the unpardonable sin of that particular office, that to give the required address meant official decapi-tation, if 'hari kari' on the part of the offender did not intervene, but that if I addressed a letter to the Admiral it would be duly forwarded."

"You did that, of course?"

"No, on the contrary I did not do it. I told the clerk that I was a Canadian, that I wanted the Admiral's address for historical purposes and that, as I was leaving for Canada immediately, he might oblige me. He said, 'You had better let me for-ward your letter; the sooner you do so the quicker you will get an answer.' I said: 'No.' I had thought of another way out. I could make no impression on the official. He was most civil—not a bad sort at all—but firm as a well-set anchor. I thought I saw the glint of a smile on his face as I turned away. Back again went I to the old quar-termaster and I quickly enlisted him in my service —for the time being anyhow. The old gentleman was quite a connoisseur in coins. He looked with the eye of an expert on a piece of gold which had been rendered valuable by the impress of the Queen's head. I went over the situation with him; opened my mind to him, and finally he suggested a letter to the Paymaster-General, adding that it would be his special care to see that I received a speedy answer. I acted as prompted. I penned my request, enclosed my card, told the old quarter-master that in my opinion he should be an Admiral, and that my influence was at his service if he would but get me the coveted answer, and that I would be back in an hour.

"'I'll do my best for you sir. I can't do more—but give me an hour and a half.'

"I readily agreed and awaited results. I passed an hour and a half in the gallery of the House of Commons, listening, I remember, to an impertinent Scotch member baiting a Government postoffice official about the 'wretched mail service in the north of Scotland.' The Scotchman made the official promise a better service. This was on a Wednesday and I had to leave for Liverpool at midnight on Friday to catch the steamer—and if successful I wanted to have a reply from the Admiral."

"I fancy you got what you wanted?"

"I did, but not as readily as you might suppose."

"Why, didn't your letter bring a reply?"

"Yes, it did, but not at the first call. I went back to the Admiralty and found that no answer had arrived, that I must call later in the day, and even then there was no certainty of a favourable reply, for my first effort and non-success were well-known to the old quartermaster. Finally, I made a last call. It looked like a forlorn hope to me, but it would never do to give up."

"Did you go back the same day?"

"The same day—yes, within the appointed time. My naval friend said that no letter had yet arrived, but that he expected one shortly. He called one of half-a-dozen old seamen who were acting as messengers in the waiting-room and sent him off to the Paymaster's office—but without result. A second man was posted off ten minutes later, but he, too, came back empty-handed. Then after a second interval of ten minutes a third was sent out with an extra special order whispered in his ear. This veteran, who wore medals, had luck on his side—luck for both of us. He brought back a dozen letters—surely one was for me. The old quartermaster examined them and finally picked out one and handed it to another seaman-messenger, directed him to a room leading off the waiting-room. Back came the messenger with the information that the official named was not in his room and that the behest of the quartermaster could not be attended to. The old gentleman was my friend. He gave another order—to the same man —but to another room, and in less than two minutes he returned smiling as if he had received an increase in his pension. The letter had evidently passed before the proper official eye, for the envelope bore marks of an official pen, and in a moment I slipped from the envelope a sheet of official blue foolscap decorated at its head with the official seal and containing the brief, but eminently satisfactory information that 'Rear Admiral Richard Dawkins resided at Maisonette, Stoke Gabriel, Devon, England.' Thus ended the first act in my search. The next was to hear from the Admiral."

"That was no trouble, was it?"

"No, not only no trouble but a great deal of pleasure. I wrote to the Admiral that night, and by the return mail I received a kindly letter, stating that both he and his wife would be pleased to do what they could to further my desires. He added that he was an old member of the Craft and that in his dining-room at Maisonette hung an oil by Renagle, R.A., of Simon McGillivray, his father-in-law, in Masonic regalia, as Provincial Grand Master of Upper Canada, when in York in 1822."

"And we have his portrait in Toronto?"

"Yes, I had it copied in oil and it now hangs with those of Bros. Jarvis, Fitzgibbon, Beikie, Dr. Kerr, Ziba Phillips, McNab and Ridout, all past rulers of the Craft, presented by me to the Masonic Hall Trust in the Temple building."

"It must have gratified the Admiral and his wife?"

"Yes, and all their family. I spent some pleasant days at Maisonette every year after that of my find. The Admiral was a courteous old gentleman, hospitable and entertaining—a true type of the British sailor. He predeceased his wife. Mrs. Dawkins, Simon McGillivray's only child, died three years ago. She was a devoted wife and mother, and one of my delights during the few years 1 had the pleasure of her acquaintance, was to hear her recount all that she had heard of her father from members of the family who survived him, for Mrs. Dawkins was born seven months after her father's death. McGillivray was a highly educated and travelled man. Hundreds of pages of his writings, accounts of his travels and incidents of his life may be seen in his late daughter's home, now the residence of two grand-daughters and two grandsons, one of whom, a bright boy of twelve, is proud of his name, John McGillivray Dawkins. That is how I found McGillivray. It is just sixty years ago next Saturday, the 9th of June, since Simon McGillivray was put away in the family vault of the Easthope family, in Norwood Cemetery, near London. He was comparatively young—fifty-five years of age. Mrs. Dawkins told me that very often the Duke of Sussex would drive down to the city and spend an evening with her father in Suffolk Lane."

" What about Canadian pictures? Did you have as much trouble in securing them as English ones?"

" Nearly—but I never had such a hunt as I had for McGillivray's. I found a capital oil of Bro. Jarvis, the first Provincial Grand Master, in the possession of his grandson, Bro. Æmilius Jarvis, of Toronto. It is a good example of the work of some English painter. In this oil Jarvis is garbed as an officer of the Queen's Rangers. There is also a pencil sketch of him as he sat in the Grand Lodge at York (Toronto) in 1804. That has been enlarged and is now in oil in the Craft room of the Temple building in Toronto. This find came to hand at first call—not so Dr. Kerr's picture. Dr. Kerr was the rival of Bro. Jarvis. When the latter was P. G. M. at Niagara, Kerr was his deputy, and when in 1800-01 the Niagara brethren revolted at Jarvis' rule, Kerr grasped the gavel of the schismatic Grand Lodge in the old capital and ruled it well. Dr. Kerr was one of the best-known men at Niagara. He was surgeon of Sir John Johnson's 2nd Battalion and was surgeon to the Indian Department of Upper Canada. To find a clue to Dr. Kerr's identity was a pleasant enough, though prolonged, task. Old military documents were unearthed in the Archives Department at Ottawa. The records of St. Mark's church at Niagara were read line upon line; the civil records were scanned, but the results were confined to a statement of offices, both military and civil, held from 1792-1823.

"I found that his wife, who was a daughter of Sir William Johnson, by his second wife, Molly Brant, died in 1794, and was buried in St. Mark's churchyard. Her tomb is there to this day. But of Dr. Kerr, old Niagarians knew little if anything. One old lady, who passed away some years ago, said that Dr. Kerr used to come to her father's house in 1820, when she was but seven years of age, and she thought a daughter of Dr. Kerr had married a Gillespie, but where he lived or what he did she knew not, but he had left Niagara in 1823. This was a clue, slight indeed, but of value. I knew that there was only one family of the name of Gillespie in Canada likely to be connected with Dr. Kerr and that was the Gillespies of Montreal. The first post carried a letter to M. W. Bro. A. A. Stevenson, of Montreal, with a request that he would enquire of the Gillespies of that city and report. Bro. Stevenson performed ʰˑˑ mission promptly. But then the Colonel is always prompt and obliging. Do you know that Bro. Alex. Mitchell and Bro. Stevenson are really the only

living links left between the present genera-
tion of Craftsmen and those who took an active
part in Quebec at the time of the union of the
Grand Lodges in 1858. The return mail brought
word that Dr. Kerr was the son-in-law of Sir
William Johnson, but that no picture of him
existed. If so, it was not on this side of the
Atlantic; it might be on the other side. Sir
Edward Gillespie, of Lombard street, London, England, was written to. He replied that his aunt was
a daughter of Dr. Kerr, but that a picture of him
had never been made. Shattered hopes again—
the most energetic Mason of 1792-1822—all of his
work but nothing of his form. It seemed as if the
Craft would never view the face of the Masonic
master mind of the first quarter of the century. But
fortune favoured me, as it often has, and the next
mail brought the welcome news that a miniature on
ivory had been discovered by Sir Edward Gillespie.
So the picture was found and its replica in oil, life
size, hangs on the walls of the Blue Room in the
Temple building, Toronto."

"I suppose you had many other experiences in
securing engravings to illustrate your book?"

"Yes, many; about a legion. The coin chapter
gave me no end of trouble. Many of the coins
were out of the 'boxes' of the old lodges. Some
came from a chest of one of the Niagara lodges, as
for instance, the half-penny of George III. and the
U. S. dollar of 1799. The French ecu or crown
given, belonged to the Merchants' Lodge, of Quebec, 1764-70. It was one of the reign of Louis XIV.
The army bills and bills of exchange are from the
collection of Bro. Dr. Neilson, Surgeon-General of
Canada. The Pretended Bank of Upper Canada
bills are also his. But I had one belonging to the
Grand Lodge of 1822-26, which had been paid to
Bro. John Dean, Grand Secretary, by some of the
Kingston lodges. I have reproduced two beautiful

views of the old city from the five and ten dollar bills of the Pretended Bank of Upper Canada, which are owned by Bro. Neilson. The U. S. cent of 1796 belonged to lodge No. 12, Stamford. The Bank of England dollar belonged to Bro. William Jarvis. By the way, the early bills of exchange drawn by Jarvis were unique. The French franc of 1806 belonged to a French trader who was a member of Adoniram Lodge in Amherstburg, and the Brock half-piece of 1816, and the same coin of Upper Canada, 1812, yes, and I think the same coin of 1816, were picked up from the family of a descendant of an old treasurer of Rideau, the lodge at Burritt's Rapids, which met as early as 1815-22. The table I have given in that chapter I compiled when I was on a trip to the West Indies in 1896. I gave a couple of hours a day to it for nearly two weeks. I had it revised by Mr. Scott and Mr. Haydn Horsey, of the Dominion Bank, Toronto, who were also on that trip. The table shows the value of all the coins in sterling, Halifax, New York and Canadian currency from 1777-1899."

"What a rare set of plates you have of the Goose and Gridiron Tavern."

"Yes, I have to thank Messrs. Searle & Hay, the architects, of Ludgate Hill, for those elevations, and Bro. Arthur Greenwood, of Bermondsey, S.E., the contractor who pulled down the old tavern and built the new warehouse on the site. He it was who gave me the bits of timber from the rafters which supported the floor of the room where the Masons met in 1717. I actually found in the cellar under the bar Indian coins of about 1400 or 1500, and a half-pence of 1717-19, dropped through some hole in th    oor by a not over careful barmaid. I failed to fir   'ictures of all the taverns where the Grand Lodge  .' England met, but of the Turk's Head in Greek St, Soho, I found a sketch of part of the public room. There are no pictures of the Rummer and Grapes Tavern, Canon Row, Westminster, extant; nor of the Crown, in Parker St., Drury Lane, nor of the famous Apple Tree Tavern, in Charles street, Covent Garden. At the Turk's Head the Grand Lodge of the Ancients was formed in 1751, and at the others the ' Four Old Lodges ' met.

" In my seal chapter I had quite a time to find the first seal of the Grand Lodge of Canada, 1855. I forget where I found it, but I think it was on a document issued to either No. 20 or No. 209a in London by Bro. T. B. Harris, the Grand Secretary of the period.

" It would take too long to tell you of the chase which Bro. Ehlers, the Grand Secretary of New York and I had for the warrants of the Detroit lodges of 1764 and 1794. Bro. Ehlers used to declare to me that he never had had the document, but Bro. John Barker and Bro. Herman Carter both declared that it was in the archives of New York. One day a literary Mason called on Ehlers. They chatted about Masonry and its history. No one can talk on that subject better than Ehlers. Well, in the course of the conversation Ehlers told his literary caller that the Grand Lodge of New York was the only organization of the kind that could show a provincial warrant. ' Indeed,' said the brother, ' where is it?' Off Ehlers posted to the safe and opening an envelope took from it the provincial warrant of New York of about 1785, and as he opened it to display it, out dropped the Detroit warrant of 1764. It was months before the gallant colonel recovered from the surprise. The old warrant had been there for many years. 1 ` Grand Lodge of New York has sent the venerable document to Zion Lodge at Detroit, and also the Lower Canada warrant of 1794, which had been granted in that year by Thomas Ainslie, the D G.M. of Lower Canada when Prince Edward. father of our Queen, was G.M.

" The fact is that there is some incident con-
nccted with every one of the five hundred pictures
in the two volumes of my history. In some in-
stances I failed to find other pictures that I
wanted. For instance, I have searched the world
over for a portrait of General Simon Fraser, who
led the Highlanders at Louisbourg and was with
Wolfe at Quebec. He was the eldest son by the
first wife, of Lord Lovat, who was beheaded in
1747. The picture of his half-brother, Archibald,
is offered for sale frequently as that of Simon
Fraser. There is another picture that I wanted,
that of Col. Christopher Carleton, nephew of Sir
Guy Carleton. He was in the 29th Foot and died at
Quebec in 1785. Then another face I would like to
have had is that of Bro. Thos. Carleton, the first
Governor of New Brunswick and also that of the
Hon. Edward Cornwallis, uncle of Lord Cornwallis, who surrendered at Yorktown. These
three pictures will not, I suppose, ever be
found. We have those of all of the P. G. M.'s
of Upper Canada, but only of one Grand
Secretary, Bro. Turquand, who held that office
from 1822-1830. That of Bro. Sylvcster Tiffany of 1792 I cannot find, although his direct descendant, Bro. E. H. Tiffany, of Alexandria, Ont.,
has made every search for it. Neither has the
picture of Bro. Davenport Phelps been found. but
I have some hopes of it turning up some day.
Phelps was the first Grand Secretary under Jarvis.
The Hon. Robert Hamilton's picture is not to the
fore. He was the G. S. W. under Jarvis. Thanks
to Bro. Dunstan of the Bell Telephone Company, I have a fine picture of R. W. Bro.
Thomas Adams. a very worthy man. who was
the last of the Provincial Grand Masters of the
Niagara Grand Lodge. Bro. Dunstan's wife is a
granddaughter of Bro. Adams. Bro. George For-
syth's face is another one missing from the list.

MSS. come one's way. You are on the lookout but don't find ; then some day you get a hint and follow up a trail, just as I did late one winter night when I found in a farmhouse some miles from Toronto the Jarvis warrant of 1792, and the minute books of the Niagara ..ges from 1795-1822. Yes, I called on Bro. George Bennett the next morning at two o'clock and wakened him up to show him the warrant and MSS. for which we had searched all over Canada, England and the United States for nearly twenty years. The warrant and the MSS. had been locked away ever since 1817 when Jarvis died—just eighty-three years ago in 1900."

CPSIA information can be obtained
at www.ICGtesting.com
Printed in the USA
BVHW041042170119
538075BV00017B/886/P